Totally Me!

A Girl's Handbook and Journal

Charlotte Houston

Scholastic Inc.

New York   Toronto   London   Auckland   Sydney
Mexico City   New Delhi   Hong Kong   Buenos Aires

Before using any of the health and beauty recipes in this book,
first test a little on your skin or hair.

ISBN 0-439-55104-8

Text © 2002 Charlotte Houston.
Illustrations © 2002 by Jessie Eccles.

All rights reserved. Published by Scholastic Inc., 557 Broadway, New York, NY
10012, by arrangement with The Chicken House.

12 11 10 9 8 7 6 5 4 3 2   3 4 5 6 7 8/0

Printed in the U.S.A.
First Scholastic Printing,
September 2003
Designed by Alison Withey

Totally Me!

Name . . . .

Contents

Introduction

Congratulations! Not only have you just picked up the greatest book ever written for girls, but by forking out the money for this book, I'm guessing that you're a girl — and that's *really* something to celebrate!

For starters, we girls get to do lots of things that boys don't. I'm talking about wearing fabulous clothes, gossiping for hours, and plastering our rooms with pictures of our best friends and fave bands. OK, so there are some things that aren't so great, too, like getting zits and arguing with parents, but the beauty of this book is that it's here for your good times and your not-so-good times. Think of it as a friend that will cheer you up if you feel down, answer your questions, and give you something to do when you're bored. Because, let's face it — there's only so much on TV a girl can watch before going cross-eyed!

Totally Me! is divided into eight chapters and each one of them addresses a different part of your life (school, family, spare time . . .). Each chapter is packed with advice, stories, info, and things to make you laugh out loud. Look for the boredom busters — these are ideas for cool activities. They might tell you how to make something, suggest a fun game, or give tips for relaxing. Plus, there's even a fortune-teller to help see where your life's going. Cool, right?

But the best thing about this book is that it's yours. And, like you, it's totally unique. No two copies of *Totally Me!* are the same. Why? Because as you're reading this book you'll be asked to fill in special journal sections called *My Moments*. You'll have room to write down what you think, draw pictures of your friends, stick in funny photos of yourself, and fill in wacky questionnaires. Then, when you've finished reading the book, not only will you be a total girl expert, you'll have your very own journal, too!

So, now that you've made the best decision of your life and bought *Totally Me!*, make the next best one and start reading!

Read it, write it — and keep it forever!

The girl mantra

These are phrases that you should repeat aloud to yourself when you're feeling upset, confused, or alone. Copy them down and stick them on your mirror to help you remember them.

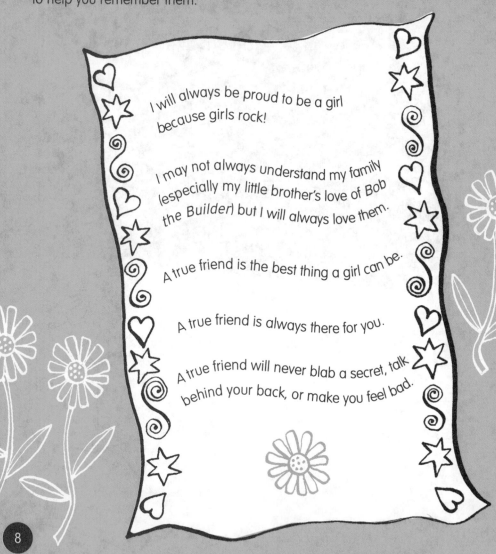

I will always be proud to be a girl because girls rock!

I may not always understand my family (especially my little brother's love of Bob the Builder) but I will always love them.

A true friend is the best thing a girl can be.

A true friend is always there for you.

A true friend will never blab a secret, talk behind your back, or make you feel bad.

I will always try my hardest in everything I do . . .

. . . and have a great laugh at the same time.

I will never get upset because I don't have Britney's hair or J-Lo's face, because I'm me . . .

. . . and that's the best thing I can be!

My Moments

My name is Ashley

My address is 4960 Corkwood Dr.

I am ⬜ 11 years, ⬜ 8 months, and ⬜ days old.

My birthday is April 20 1993

My three wishes would be

When I grow up I want to be

Here are 20 words totally about me

I <u>started</u> writing, sketching, drawing, and coloring in this
book on. . . . .

I look like this on a good day:

I look like this on a bad day:

CHAPTER 1

Your family

You can choose your friends, but you can't choose your family.

They're the first people you see in the morning and the last people you see at night. They look after you when you're sick, show you how to ride a bike, and make you feel all warm and cozy when they give you a hug. They can also bug you more than nails on a chalkboard. What are they? Your family.

But, relax . . . if your family didn't get on your nerves sometimes, then they wouldn't be normal. It's part of their job description. And I'll let you in on another secret. You know that perfect family you see in ads? You know . . . smiling, tanned mom and dad, white-teethed children, and a dog? They don't exist. Of course, sometimes your family does seem totally perfect, but then your dad paints the bathroom the wrong color, your mom gets mad and starts crying, your sister shaves off all her hair, and your little brother smashes the antique vase in the front room. Arrrgh!

What I'm trying to say is that although *The Simpsons* is just a cartoon, every family has "naughty Bart" moments and "embarrassing Homer" moments. We wouldn't be human if we didn't. But our families do love us, and if it weren't for our parents, none of us would be here. And life would be pretty boring if it was like the commercials all the time, wouldn't it? Besides, are anyone's teeth *really* that white?

Family Fun

Some people think your position in the family affects what kind of person you are. Check our chart to see if it's true for you. . . .

Oldest kids are . . .

. . . really ambitious. They know what they want and they go out and get it. They're also total perfectionists, so everything in their bedroom will be neatly in its place and their wardrobe's probably color coordinated. They're bossy, don't like admitting they're wrong, and can be a bit serious. They make great, caring friends but could do with lightening up a bit.

Middle kids are . . .

. . . really friendly and chatty. They love meeting new people and are really generous. Great if they have a huge chocolate bar! They don't like arguing and could even be tempted to lie if it stops a fight. They're hardworking and fair but have a competitive streak and hate losing.

Youngest kids are . . .

. . . fun troublemakers. They love taking risks, they're outgoing, and they can be very funny. They absolutely love being the center of attention, but they can sometimes be hurtful when they think they're just fooling around. They make great friends but can let you down.

"Because I said so…"

Don't you just hate it when your parents say that? Why do they say it so much when they know it makes you sooo crazy? The reason is . . . because they can.

When your parents won't let you do something, it can be *totally* frustrating. But although you may think, *It's only Lyndsey's party!* you have to remember that parents operate on a whole other level and their brains work in different ways. They may have lots of reasons for not wanting you to go, like:

They can't take you and are worried that you'll get lost if you go on your own.

They don't know Lyndsey or her parents and she could be, like, an ax-murderer or something.

You haven't eaten anything and could collapse from exhaustion when you get there. And that would make your mom look really bad. . . .

You've got homework to do.

They want to spend some time with their daughter.

Frankly, it could be any reason on earth, but they are usually only thinking of what's best for you. At the time, you may think your parents are being selfish and unfair, but they're not!

Top 5 things parents always say

— and what they really mean. . . .

Just to show that it's not just your parents who say it.

Because I said so . . .

"I haven't got time to discuss this now."

"Do you have to copy everything that Lyndsey does?"

And if Lyndsey jumped off a bridge, I suppose you would, too?

I don't care what Lyndsey's parents let her do.

"You're not doing it."

"I'm in charge here— and don't you forget it."

While you're living under my roof you'll do as I say.

Whaddya think I am, made of money?

"You're not getting any more cash!"

'Rent control

The best way to get your parents on your side is to act older than your age and talk about the problem. If it helps, you could even write down your feelings and show the note to your parents. Compromise is another trick that will help you. So, if you want to stay out until 9 P.M., but your mom wants you back at 8, then suggest you'll be back at 8:30 and see what she says. Once you've shown that you can be trusted to get in at 8:30 a few times, maybe she'll let you stay out till 9? And although it might be tempting to lie to them ("Yes, of course, I've done my homework!"), it's not worth it. Parents have built-in lie detectors and your plan will be foiled. Don't ask me how they know when you're stretching the truth, but they do — believe me!

> "My mom and dad are sooooo strict. They won't let me play with my friends till I've done my homework and helped with the housework. It's really annoying."
> Hayley (12)

Too cool for rules?

Most parents have some kind of rules that they expect you to follow, like what time you have to go to bed or what chores you have to help with. But it's not just parents that make you stick to rules. Bet your school has certain rules that you have to stick to. And no matter what job you do in the future, you'll have to follow rules, too.

> "Rules are dumb. I don't see the point of them. They just stop you from having fun."
> Emma (9)

Family rules are supposed to be there to make life easier (sometimes for you and sometimes for them). If your parents won't let you go into town on your own until you're a teenager, it's because they're worried about you. And if they say you can't blast your CDs after 8:00 p.m., it's probably because your music is too loud for them to hear the TV. So, unfortunately, the only way to deal with house rules is to follow them. It will make life easier for you (there'll be less arguing and sulking) and it's good life practice (if you don't follow rules at work, you won't get paid). If you really, really think it's unfair that you have to help your dad wash the car on Sundays then offer to do something else instead.

Stain, stain, go away . . .

Doing chores around the house can be boring, hard work, and take up lots of time but, like homework, it won't do itself. (Wouldn't that be a great invention, though? I think I'm gonna start working on it now.) And let's just be thankful that we weren't born a few hundred years ago when "a woman's work was never done" and looking after the house, cleaning, and cooking was all we girls were allowed to do. Nowadays, with dish-washers and washing machines, things don't take as long as they used to. Best of all, it's not just the girls who cook and clean in the 21st century. So, if your bro gets to watch TV while you have to polish, drop a polite word in the 'rents' ears and tell them that we're not in the Dark Ages anymore!

Oh, brother . . .

You may spend half your life moaning about how long your older sister spends in the bathroom, but having brothers and sisters is all about that word again — *compromise*. You may be totally different from your siblings (they're good at drawing and you hate it, or they love Eminem and you hate him) but they're still family. And there may be times in the future when your brother helps you out or your sister moves away and you really miss her. So try and enjoy the time you have together. If they're older than you, they may be able to help you by telling you what it's like to be 14 years old. If they're younger, you can help *them*. Having siblings gives you practice dealing with other people and caring and sharing. It's not always gonna be easy, but hey, who said life was easy?

5 things to do with your brothers and sisters

— when they're not driving you crazy. . . .

❋ Go through your closets and dress up in each other's clothes.

❋ Put on plays and performances for your parents.

❋ Organize a sports day in the backyard or park — tennis, running, egg 'n' spoon, and sack races.

❋ Build a tent outside and take some food, books, and toys with you. Escape the 'rents for hours!

❋ Make a set of drums out of a few cans and start a family band. This one will *really* please the 'rents!

So there you have it — your total guide to families. No matter how big or small they are, they'll always be a huge part of your life and no matter how much they annoy you (and they will annoy you) they'll always be there for you.

Ask Away!

Dear *TM*,
My dad is always telling me off for small things and he won't let me wear fashionable clothes or makeup. What can I do?

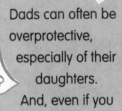

Dads can often be overprotective, especially of their daughters. And, even if you don't feel like one, he probably still thinks of you as his little girl. Why not try talking to your mom or another close relative if it's really upsetting you? Then maybe they'll have a quiet word with him and you'll feel a lot better for getting your feelings off your chest. I'm sure your dad has your best interests at heart, so try not to get too upset about it. Remember that by dealing with this maturely, your dad will realize that you're growing up and won't be his little girl forever.

Ask Away!

Dear *TM*,
My parents are always arguing – they say really nasty things to each other. Why do they do this? Are they gonna get divorced?

Although we sometimes think our parents know everything and never make mistakes, they're only human. Sometimes they argue, cry, and sulk just like us. But if the arguing is happening a lot and it's upsetting you, try to talk to them about it. Once you've let them know how upset you are, maybe your parents will try to control their arguing. I don't know if they're going to get divorced, but although it's a scary word, sometimes people are happier apart than they are together. And remember — no matter how much your parents fight with each other, they will *always* love you.

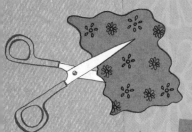

Boredom Busters

Draw your family tree.
This will take a lot of research and may mean asking your parents and grandparents all about their relatives. See how far back in time you can trace your roots.

Plan your dream family vacation.
- Where would you go?
- Who would you take with you?
- What would your hotel be like and what would you do?
- Try making a vacation brochure or designing some postcards.

Slumber Athletics
Build an obstacle course in your bedroom with chairs, boxes, and pillows to climb over. Now zip yourself into a sleeping bag and start wiggling. Get your brother or sister to time you as you go around, and hold a family contest.

Reinvent your room.

There are lots of things you can do to your room to make it unique and give it that personal touch. You could cut out posters and pics of your fave celeb and make a poster wall. Or you could try making funky pillow covers.

Here's how:

1. Buy some fabric in a cool print like leopard skin or polka dot (you could even use old clothes).
2. Cut 2 identical shapes out of your fabric — heart shapes work well.
3. Put the fabric back-to-back so the nice side is on the inside.
4. Sew around the edges, leaving a small gap for stuffing.
5. Turn your shape the right side out and stuff with cotton batting or old tights until the cushion is plump.
6. Sew up the gap.

Now make more matching pillows!

My Moments

Mom

Name . . . .
Age . . . .
Birthday . . . .
Star sign . . . .
Fave Food . . . .
Fave TV show . . . .

Nickname for me . . . .
Fave saying . . . .

I love them because

Dad

. . . .
. . . .
. . . .
. . . .
. . . .
. . . .

. . . .
. . . .

Sister/Brother

Name . . . Michelle . . . .
Age . . . . 9 . . . .
Birthday . 5/15/95 . . . .
Star sign . . . .
Fave Food . . . .
Fave TV show . . . .

Nickname for me . . . .
Fave saying . . . .

I love them because

Sister/Brother

. . . Ben . . . .
. . . .
5/22/98 . . . .

24

Here's a photo of me with my family:

The best thing about my family is . . . .
. . . .
. . . .

The worst thing about my family is . . . .
. . . .
. . . .

Our best family vacation was . . . .
. . . .
. . . .

CHAPTER 2

Your friends

A friend is someone who thinks you're a good egg even if you're slightly cracked.

Who's the first person you want to talk to if you've just heard Justin's new single? Or if you've just bought those cool jeans from the Gap that you've been saving for since Christmas? Your bud, of course. It could be your BFF, a pal from dance class, or a girl you just met. But how do you make friends? Can a gal ever have too many friends? And what's the best way to cope if you and your pal fight? Don't sweat it — we'll talk about all these things later. First, here are the ten rules of friendship that every girl should learn. How many can you check off for your BFF?

- ✓ A good friend doesn't gossip or spread rumors.
- A good friend never judges you (if you think Pacey's cuter than Dawson, she'll accept that).
- A good friend will never lie to you (even if it means telling you that those pink shorts look totally awful).
- A good friend will never drop you for someone else.
- A good friend will always share her chocolate, clothes, and CDs.
- A good friend will never be too busy for you.
- A good friend will love you for who you are, **not** because she wants a turn on your computer!
- A good friend will laugh **with** you, not **at** you.
- A good friend will have shoulders big enough for you to cry on whenever you need to.
- A good friend can be trusted with your money, your clothes . . . with you!

That's what friends are for

Who needs friends when they have ice cream? Well . . . everyone, actually. Because no matter how big your pile of ice cream, it won't lend you the new Kylie CD or cheer you up if you've just had an argument with your mom. All girls need a group of friends to hang with. OK, brothers and sisters can be cool, but not *all* the time.

"My best friends are named Laura and Jody. We always hang out together and they're just like my sisters 'cause they know me so well."

Emma (12)

Meeting friends

It's easy to meet new friends at school (they don't have to be in your class), in your street or town, at the swimming pool, in the park . . . the list goes on. Basically, anywhere that you like to hang out, other kids your age will probably hang out, too. So next time you see someone that you think you'd like to get to know, try giving them a smile and saying hi. If they don't reply or aren't interested, then don't push it. But if they smile back, then try making conversation.

You can talk about anything — last night's *Simpsons*, the new teacher at school, or the sneakers she's wearing. As you talk, you may discover that you have things in common. This is the main way people make their friends — shared interests. It could be chocolate ice cream or it could be gymnastics, but once you've found that you like the same kind of stuff, you'll never run out of things to say and your phone bill will never be the same again — ooooops!

"My friend is just the best. She knows what to say when I'm upset and we have fun together all the time."

Fiona (9)

Quiz — What type of friend is she?

Take this quiz to discover if your bud's totally great or totally terrible!

1 You invite your friend over to listen to CDs and try on your new clothes. What does she do?

A. Comes over, stays for an hour, and leaves with your J-Lo video and new hair clips.

B. Races straight over, bringing her new Pink CD to get the party started.

C. Comes over with her mom's makeup that she's borrowed to convince you that thick black eyeliner is cool.

2 It's the school dance and you decide to try out the new Britney routine. What does your pal do?

A. Joins in at once. Even though you haven't got the steps right, you both have a great laugh.

B. Dances a few steps but dashes off to talk to another friend a few minutes later.

C. Points and laughs as soon as you go on the dance floor, then says, "I don't know what *your* problem is!" when you get back.

3 Your mom says that you can go over to your friend's house as long as you don't go to the park and are back for dinner. What does your bud say?

A. "You must be kidding! We're meeting the guys in five minutes at the park. Don't be a loser *all* your life."

B. "Cool. Let's just stay in and practice that Britney routine."

C. "OK. Don't bother coming over, then. See you tomorrow."

4 You've just learned some quality gossip about Loopy Linda from down the block. You tell your friend and swear her to secrecy. What does she do?

A. Tells a few people, but swears them to secrecy, too.

B. Tells no one, but has a good giggle about it.

C. Tells your class, your entire street, and Mrs. Hague the hairdresser, too.

5 Do you get along well with all of your friend's friends?

A. No way. Your parents won't even let you hang around with some of them.

B. Yes, most of them.

C. She's got so many of them that you can't keep up. Anyway, she doesn't introduce you to many of them.

Answers

1	A. 1	B. 3	C. 2
2	A. 3	B. 2	C. 1
3	A. 1	B. 3	C. 2
4	A. 2	B. 3	C. 1
5	A. 1	B. 3	C. 2

Conclusions

Best Bud (11–15)

She's a fab friend who you can really trust. She's a joker but knows when to be serious, too. Your friendship is totally give-and-take and she's a real cutie — worth hanging on to!

Part-time Pal (7–11)

She's a good friend but she's kinda selfish, too. She'll take what she can from you and not always offer much in return. She's got tons of friends, so don't expect this girl's total attention 24/7. Have fun when you're with her, but make sure you have other pals, too.

Bad Babe (under 7)

This girl is not your friend but she pretends she is. She may seem cool and fun to be around, but she'll end up getting you in trouble. She doesn't have true friends, just people who are scared of her or put up with her. Don't be one of them!

"Make friends, make friends, never, never break friends."

It's very rare that two friends *never* fight. There can be all sorts of reasons for this — jealousy, other friends, and gossip are some of the most common. But whatever the reason, one thing's for certain — no one likes fighting with their friend. It's horrible!

Dealing with an argument

First of all, you need to cool off. Once you've calmed down, you'll be able to decide what you should do next. If you really, really don't think the argument was your fault, try asking someone who you can really trust to talk to your friend for you. Or send her a note or an e-mail. It's less stressful than meeting face-to-face, but will show that you're thinking of her. If she doesn't respond, then leave it for a while. She needs time to chill out, too.

"I hate arguing with my friends and try hard not to. If we do argue, I'm always the one to try and make up first 'cause I hate fighting so much."

Fiona (10)

"I'm stubborn and never really want to apologize. But being lonely is so upsetting that I just send my friend a note and hope we'll make up. We only argue about silly things like homework, anyway."

Hayley (12)

Eventually there will come a time when you can talk, cry, or laugh about the argument — and there's nothing more fun than making up. Here's some argument advice from someone who's had far too many of them in her life!

Do

- Take deep breaths and try to calm down. You don't want to say something that you don't really mean and will totally regret.
- Try to put yourself in your friend's position and understand her point of view.
- If you feel bad, make her something or write her a cute poem.
- Understand that there are some things you may never agree on and that they're not worth arguing about.
- When you're alone, cry, scream, or shout — if it makes you feel better.

Don't

- Hit, punch, or hurt your friend. Violence will get you nowhere and will only make you feel bad about yourself.
- Be stubborn. If she's making an effort, you should, too.
- Tell your group what a witch she's been and turn them all against her.
- Be mean to her or ignore her if she tries to make up with you.
- Take it out on your family or other friends. You need all the support you can get!

Pressure?

Having a group of friends can be the best feeling in the world — and it can also be the worst. Just because you hang out in a group doesn't mean you're the same kind of people. What's right for one girl might not be right for you. Although you're part of a group, you're also a unique person with your own personality and beliefs. So don't feel bad about not joining in if you don't want to. If everyone thinks it's cool to bully the new girl and you don't, then speak up. Or if you're too shy to do this, walk away and show them that you're not comfortable with the situation.

Peer pressure is when you feel like you should be doing something because everyone else is. But you don't have to do anything that you don't want to. Remind your friends of this if they're pushing you into something. If they continue forcing you, they're not true friends and it's time to think seriously about dumping them. You have the power to make your own choices, so don't be afraid to stand out from the crowd!

Boy friend or boyfriend?

You may have lots of friends that are boys — or you might just think *Gross*! But whatever your view, as you get older, you may find that your thoughts about boys get more serious — slushy and stuff. But boys *can* make great friends, so for now just enjoy spending time with them!

Ask Away!

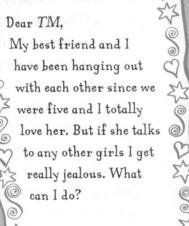

Dear *TM*,
My best friend and I
have been hanging out
with each other since we
were five and I totally
love her. But if she talks
to any other girls I get
really jealous. What
can I do?

Wow, you're obviously great friends if you've known each other
since you were little, so you must be pretty good at sharing
secrets. It's time to tell her how you feel. Jealousy isn't a very nice
emotion, but it's one that everyone suffers from every now and
then. Maybe she feels the same when you talk to other people.
I'm sure she'll tell you that even though she's got other friends
and interests, you're her BFF — and that will never change. It's
completely natural to feel upset but I'm sure after a chat with her
your mind will be put at rest. Anyway, you wouldn't want her to be
sitting around on her own while you're at dance class, would you?

Ask Away!

Dear *TM*,
My friend is really starting to get me down. She's always being mean to me and telling people my secrets. Is she just joking around?

Your friend might think that she's just being funny, but she isn't. Tell her how she's making you feel and that you want it to stop. It sounds like she might be jealous of you and that's why she's trying to make you look bad. Have a chat with her to try to find out the reasons for her behavior. If talking doesn't work, then it's time to walk away from her and her bullying ways for good.

Boredom Busters

Show your friend how much she means to you by making her this cool **friendship bracelet**. Then, every time she puts it on, she'll think of you. You'll need five different colored pieces of thread, a ruler, scissors, and a large needle and safety pin.

1. Measure and cut the colored threads into 32-inch pieces.

2. Knot them together 2 inches from one end and put the safety pin through the knot. This will stop it from twisting.

3. Pull thread 2 tight, make a loop around it with thread 1, and pull into a knot. Make another loop the same way.

4. Hold thread 3 tight and knot the thread you just made over it twice. Repeat on threads 4 and 5 until the thread you first made is right at the back and has been knotted around all the threads.

5. Repeat steps 2 and 3 using the thread nearest to you (2). Like you did before, knot it twice around each of the other threads till it gets right to the back.

6. Once you think it's long enough, tie all the threads together and trim.

If you get really good at this, try threading on beads every 10 rows.

Slammin' Sleepover

Organize the best sleepover ever! Or, if you're not allowed to have one, offer to organize a sleepover for your friend. That's what friends are for! Here are some tips:

- Think of a theme, e.g. the Wild West, pop stars . . .
- Design the invites to fit in with your theme (so if it's a pop-star party, you could decorate the invites with magazine pics of all your fave stars).
- Make sure your food is nibbly and fun — pizzas, chips, cheese, pineapple slices, cakes, and cookies are all fab ideas for snack food. Why not ask your guests to bring a pack of their fave cookies with them, so your mom doesn't have to buy it all?
- No sleepover is complete without cool music. Sort out your CDs before the guests arrive, or make a mix so you don't have to be DJ all night.
- See if you can rent a video or DVD and get ready to swoon over Brad Pitt or learn the dances from *Grease*.
- A disposable camera is a good idea for any party. They're not too expensive and you'll be able to look at the photos whenever you're down. You could even give framed pics to your friends.

American Idol

You've seen the show, so why not act it out? Get your friends to bring some pop-star clothes over, put the tunes on, and away you go. You can dress up as your fave star, learn the words and dance routines, and pretend you're on *Idol*. Better get practicing!

Here is a picture of me and my best friend:

My best friend is . . . .

I met her when . . . .

I think she's fab because . . . .

Her birthday is . . . .

Her star sign is . . . .

Her fave TV show is . . . .

If me and my BFF argue, the thing I miss about her the most is

. . . .

. . . .

. . . .

To make her laugh you have to . . . .
. . . .

Here's a photo of me and my friends:

My friends are . . . .
. . . .
. . . .

The things we like doing together are . . . .
. . . .
. . . .

The best sleepover we had was . . . .
. . . .

The craziest thing we ever did was . . . .
. . . .

39

CHAPTER 3

Your school

Ability can take you to the top but character keeps you there.

You know the feeling. Your alarm goes off, Mom comes into the room, and for just a few seconds you think it's Saturday and plan a day of nonstop fun. Then, as she yanks the curtain open, you realize that it's Monday morning and you've got a whole week of school ahead of you — aargh! But it's no good putting your head under the pillow 'cause you can't hide from school! And even though you might not believe it, school *can* be fun!

The thing about school is that even if it doesn't seem like it, what you're learning is really important for your future. Whether you want to act in blockbuster movies, design cool clothes, or work with animals, most jobs require *some* qualifications.

Next time you're sitting in class and daydreaming about what you've got for lunch, try feeding your brain instead. And you can never know too much. Even really old people don't know *everything* there is to know in the world about *everything*. Life is one big lesson and school is just the beginning. . . .

"Sometimes it's hard getting up so early, but once I get to school I really like it. And over school vacations I get bored and miss my friends."
Jody (12)

"I love reading and writing stories. It's best when the teacher reads to us at the end of the day."
Fiona (9)

What does the future hold?

There are lots of different types of schools. Boarding schools are where you stay overnight. They're a bit like Harry Potter's school, Hogwarts, only without the broomsticks. Boarding schools can be a lot of fun and you get to spend weekends and vacations back home with your family, so you don't miss them too much. There are other sorts of schools, too, like single-sex schools (just for girls or just for boys), religious schools, and special schools for ballerinas, actors, and musicians. But no matter what type of school you go to, you'll have fun, get to meet a bunch of people, and prepare for your future — all at the same time!

Although you shouldn't be worrying about it just yet, it's never too early to start thinking about what you want to be when you grow up. Do you cook creative foods, like all those TV chefs that the 'rents love watching? Would you like to work with animals? Or perhaps you think you could be a fashion designer and make swanky clothes for celebrities? There are so many choices nowadays — and you can do whatever you want to do! So, what do *you* want to do?

> "I got an A for my last writing assignment and I just couldn't believe it! I told my mom and dad as soon as I got home."
> Emma (12)

Totally Stumped

It's horrible when you get stuck on something, isn't it? How come everyone else in your class seems to understand the French homework, but to you it seems like, well . . . a different language? Chill out, *chica* — there are millions of people on this Earth and if everyone was great at the same thing, it would be a very boring place to live. But luckily it's not like that. Some people are great at drawing and might want to be an artist or sculptor when they grow up. Some may love math and science, and become famous researchers or cure diseases. When I was at school I couldn't draw, but I really liked English — especially writing stories. I even thought that I'd love to write a book someday! So, if anyone ever tells you that dreams don't come true, don't believe them. You can get whatever you want if you put your heart into it! And no matter what people tell you, you don't have to be perfect at everything. Everyone is good at something!

> "The worst thing about school is history. I just don't get it and sometimes it makes me really frustrated."
> Hayley (12)

Career quiz

You've got no idea what you want to be in the future? Take our fab quiz to figure out what you're grade A at!

Do U doodle?

Yes → Do U like reading?
No → Do U like being outside?

Do U like reading?
No → R U a 'puter techie?
Yes ↓

Do U like being outside?
No → R U a 'puter techie?
Yes ↓

Do U find it hard to concentrate?
No → R U a 'puter techie?
Yes ↓

R U a 'puter techie?
Yes → R U interested in animals?
No → Do U like learning about other countries?

R U interested in animals?
No → Do U like learning about other countries?
Yes ↓

Do U make things in your spare time?
Yes ↓
No →

Do U like learning about other countries?
Yes ↓
No →

R U interested in how other things work?
No →

Do U have a good imagination?
No → Do U like solving problems?
Yes ↓

Do U like solving problems?
No → Would U like to travel?
Yes ↓

Would U like to travel?
No →
Yes ↓

Would U like to work in a lab?
Yes ↓
No →

R U interested in health and fitness?
No →
Yes ↓

Arty Anna

Mathematical 'Manda

Language Lyndsey

Scientist Susie

Sporty Sam

Arty Anna

You're a very creative chick and like to let your imagination run wild. You're most suited to doing something like drawing or writing where you don't have to follow strict rules and can create something of your own, like a painting or a poem.

Mathematical 'Manda

You are very logical and practical. You don't like fooling around; you just want a yes or no answer to everything. You'd be great in the business world or working with computers.

Language Lyndsey

You have a knack for picking up languages and are really interested in other countries and traveling. You're a great communicator, too, and would be a fab tour guide, travel agent, or interpreter.

Scientist Susie

Put you in a white coat with some plastic glasses and you're happy. You love taking things apart, knowing how things work, and mixing up weird creations and potions. You'd be a great scientist, engineer, doctor, or vet.

Sporty Sam

You just love keeping fit and are always on the move. You prefer being out-doors and would make a great athlete, coach, or park ranger.

Teacher troubles

First things first. Teachers aren't put on the planet to be our friends or to make our lives easy. They're supposed to make sure that we learn. Some of them may be really nice and sweet and some of them may be strict and not so sweet. Having a good teacher can really help. You'll want to keep up with your schoolwork because you like them — and they can make a subject mega-interesting.

In the same way that having a good teacher can make you love a subject and try really hard, having a teacher you don't get along with can be a total nightmare. It can make you lose interest in a subject, rebel against the teacher, and not pay attention. If you really, really don't get along with your teacher, then you need to ask yourself why. Is it because he once caught you doing silly impressions of him and hasn't forgotten? Perhaps you should have a word with him about this, just to clear the air.

But if you don't like him because he's strict, then he's probably strict with everyone and there's not much you can do about it. If he insists on silence in his class then I guess you're just gonna have to keep your mouth shut for an hour! Or if he insists on making everyone do 20 sit-ups before gym class starts, then you're gonna have to put your sneakers on and — like the ad says — just do it!

School rocks because . . .
- You get to talk to your friends without running up the phone bill.
- You get to do fun things like sports and field trips.
- Without it you'd never get ahead in life, so you'd never make any cash, and you'd never get to do anything, and you'd be really bored. And we all love enjoying what we do, don't we?

"Mr. Chapel tells us tons of funny stories and jokes. He doesn't talk down to us and we always have big discussions and pretend we're people from the past. It's great 'cause he makes history so interesting."
Jody (13)

"There are lots of different groups in my school, like the Townies, who are into trendy clothes and pop music, or the Rockers, who like nü-metal and black clothes. I just try to be friends with everyone, no matter which group they're in."
Hayley (12)

"Sometimes people gang up against other people in the playground and call them names. I try not to get involved, unless they're calling my friends names."
Vikki (11)

In with the in crowd

When everyone's in the classroom listening to the teacher, there's no pressure to fit in with a particular group of people. But school can also be a terrible place for labels and cliquey groups. You may have heard people calling others nerds or geeks. And although the person doing the name-calling may think they're being really cool, they're not. Bullies often believe that the easiest way to make sure no one's laughing at them is to laugh at other people.

It's really hard but, like Vikki, don't get involved in nasty name-calling or playground gossiping. Try to accept everyone for who they are. If you think someone is nice and other people call her a nerd or a geek then don't take any notice — ignore them and trust your own opinion.

Beat the bully

Bullying can take many different forms. Bullies can call you names, get you into trouble, or even hit, punch, and shove you. They could even steal your money or your friends. So what should you do if someone at school is trying to make your life miserable?

First, try ignoring the bully and walking away from them. But if they're still hassling you, then the only way to deal with them is by telling someone else; the bullying won't stop unless you do. The best thing would be to tell a teacher when and where the bullying usually happens. They might then be able to catch the bully in the act, so it doesn't look like you've been tattling.

Here are some more bully busters:
• Stay in safe areas of school at recess and between classes.
• If you walk home, try to stay with other people or get someone to meet you halfway.

Test times

You may hate them and they may give you sleepless nights, but you'll probably have to take more than a few exams in your life, so here are some tips.

- ASK FOR HELP. If your teacher has explained something in class and you don't understand, ask them to run through it again, or see them after class and tell them you haven't understood. It's not nerdy, it's sensible.
- DON'T HIDE. Pretending the exam's not gonna happen won't help. Draw up a timetable, do some studying, and give it your best shot.
- REST. Don't cram studying into every minute of the day. Your brain needs a rest or it won't work as well. So chill out with a smoothie, watch MTV, and take your mind off it all.
- LOOK AFTER YOURSELF. You need to eat and sleep right to be at your best, so try to have healthy meals and exercise regularly when it's exam season.
- BE POSITIVE. Don't panic about all the things you haven't studied, just remind yourself of all the things you *have*. Thinking positive is the first step to achieving.

New girl

Going to a new school can be very scary, but everyone has to do it at some time. Leaving groups of friends can be hard but, hey, e-mail makes it easy to stay in touch. And you will find new friends, honest.

Everyone's been the new girl or boy at some time in their life and the only way to deal with it is to take a deep breath and smile. Breaking the ice is hard, but if someone has a Buffy note-book, why not ask them if they think Angel is cute? Or if you hear some-one with an Eminem cell-phone ring, tell them that you love Eminem and ask where they got it from. Making friends is scary and it takes time — but it's kinda fun, too. So next time there's a new girl in your class, imag-ine how shy she's feeling, go over and say hi, and I bet you'll have made her day.

The last lesson

So school's all about studying and getting as many A's on your report card as you can, right? Wrong. School is also about picking up other skills that you didn't even realize you were learning. Getting along with other kids shows that you have good communication skills. Asking the teacher questions gives you confidence and teaches you to be a quick thinker. And freezing your socks off on a hockey rink teaches you all about teamwork. These are all skills that you'll need in the future. So don't weigh yourself down with *too much* studying. You're learning at school even when you're not sitting at your desk! And, as the saying goes, experience is the greatest teacher.

Ask Away!

Dear *TM*,
My friend has just started to blow off school and I'm really worried about her. What can I do?

Usually when someone starts behaving weirdly, it's because they have a problem. Is your friend having trouble at home or at school? Why not try to find out what her problem is by inviting her over for pizza and a chat? If she won't tell you, and you're very worried about her, it's okay to go to a parent or a teacher for help.

Dear *TM*,
I absolutely hate school. Just the thought of it gets me down. I'm miserable every day and don't know what to do. Help!

The first thing to do is figure out why you hate school. Then you can go about getting some help. Most schools have trained experts who can talk to you about bullying or phobias, because in very extreme cases, it *is* possible to develop a school phobia. And although this may sound wonderful, it can be devastating and totally affect your confidence. Take a deep breath and tell your parents — they'd hate it if they knew how upset you are.

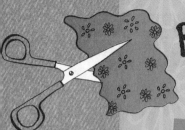

Boredom Busters

Customize your schoolbag

Who wants to have the same bag as half the school? Not you, that's for sure, so here are some ways to make your bag unique.

Lacy Lady

Get ahold of some pieces of lace from a sewing or crafts store or out of your mom's sewing box and sew them on to your bag in cool squiggles or shapes.

Braided Babe

Get six different colors of ribbon and tie them on to one of your handles in a double knot. Then braid the ribbon in the same way that you'd braid your hair and let the braids flow free.

Patchy Princess

Most accessory shops sell iron-on and sew-on patches, so get rid of that plain bag and transform it into a patchwork party!

Design a uniform

Maybe you have to wear a school uniform and hate it. Or maybe you don't have to wear one at all but wish you did. Why not try designing your own. What color would the skirt be? What style tie would you wear? It's up to you!

Make a yearbook

Take a disposable camera to school and photograph as many people as possible (even teachers!). Then dig out all your old school photos, buy yourself a big scrapbook (a regular notebook will work, too), and get to work on your very own yearbook. Design a cover using your school's emblem or the color of your uniform and write a few words about everyone inside the book. You could even get your friends to write about you.

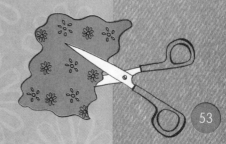

My Moments

My school is called . . . .

I'm in grade . . . .

The best things about school are . . . .

. . . .

. . . .

The things I would change about school are . . . .

. . . .

. . . .

My school colors are . . . .

Here's a list of the things I keep in my schoolbag:

My fave teacher is . . . .
. . . .

The subject I like best is . . . .
. . . .

The subject I like least is . . . .
. . . .

My fave field trip was to . . . .
. . . .
. . . .
. . . .

The best comments EVER on my report card were . . . .
. . . .
. . . .
. . . .
. . . .
. . . .

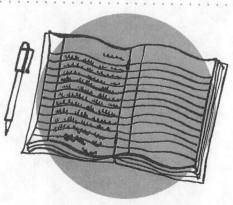

CHAPTER 4

Your health

*An apple a day
keeps the doctor away.*

When you look into the mirror, what do you see? The answer is not just a pretty, smart girl who's reading a killer book (although of course that's true!), but a unique person who has never existed before and will never exist again. There's no one quite like you in the world. There might be a girl who looks a lot like you in your school, or perhaps you and your sister look alike, but you are one of a kind and don't ever forget it!

You might not always be pleased with the way you look. Some days you may think, *My hair looks great today* or *I love my freckles,* and then a week later decide that your hair makes you look like a poodle and that you hate being freckly. Learning to love your body all the time and to take care of it is just as important as any lesson you'll learn in school. This chapter will show you how.

Fighting fit

Who doesn't love biking around with her friends and dancing along to videos on MTV? And when you do this, you're not only having fun, you're also looking after your body. Cool or what?

There are three different types of exercise and they all look after different parts of you. They are:

STRETCHING. This works your muscles and increases your flexibility. Gymnastics is a good example of a sport that uses lots of stretching.

AEROBIC. This doesn't have to mean doing jumping jacks in leg warmers. It just means making your heart beat faster. Running and tennis are both aerobic.

MUSCLE BUILDING. Unless you want to get a body like Arnold, stay away from big weights until you're much older!

Exercising is a great thing to do if you're bored, have lots of energy, or even if you're in a bad mood. Here are ten of the best.

1. **SWIMMING.** Keep fit and splash around in the water, too.
2. **RUNNING.** Racing your friends is always fun.
3. **DANCING.** Put on your fave video and practice the routines. This keeps you fit and means you'll shine like a star at the next school dance.
4. **SOCCER.** An awesome game for girls!
5. **BIKING.** Going to your pal's house will take half the time once you're on two wheels.
6. **HORSEBACK RIDING.** You don't need to own a horse to go horseback riding — there are plenty of places where you can get some saddle practice.
7. **TENNIS.** If you haven't got rackets, you and a pal may be able to rent them from the local recreation center.
8. **DOG WALKING.** It may not sound glamorous, but walking is great exercise. And your pooch will love it!
9. **SKATING.** Do it on the streets with Rollerblades or on ice. Whichever you choose, just keep your balance!
10. **KARATE.** Watch *The Karate Kid* for some inspiration and take some lessons. No one will ever disagree with you if you've got on a black belt.

You are what you eat

All that exercise is enough to make a girl eat three whopper meals a day. Great! But eating healthily is just as important as keeping fit. And although there's nothing wrong with a trip to a fast-food place every now and then, there are types of food that are much better for you and that you should try to eat every day.

FRUIT AND VEGETABLES

These contain lots of essential vitamins and minerals. Try munching on raw carrots, having fresh spinach in your salad, or making a fruit salad for dessert. There are so many types of fruits and vegetables, you're bound to find *some* you like!

CARBOHYDRATES

These give you energy and are very filling. Things like bread, rice, and pasta are all carbohydrates and are really good for your body. Brown is best in all cases as it contains more fiber. Whole-wheat bread is much tastier anyway!

DAIRY

Milk, cheese, and yogurt are all dairy foods and contain lots of calcium, which is good for your teeth and bones. There's nothing better than a glass of milk before bed. It will give you a good night's sleep, too.

PROTEIN

This is found in foods such as meat, fish, beans, and eggs; it's essential for the growth of your skin, bones, hair, and teeth. A boiled egg is a great start to the day and tuna isn't just for cats, you know!

All of these foods are good for you as long as you don't eat too much of one type. Healthy eating is all about balance. If you're a choco-holic, you may have noticed that there is something missing from the list. Other stuff we like, too, like cookies, chips, pizza, fried chicken, and burgers aren't good for us, either.

The thing is, all these types of food are very high in sugar or fat. And too much sugar or fat isn't great for you. No one's saying you can't eat them — who could live without pizza and ice cream at a sleepover? Just try not to eat too much of them. A diet of doughnuts for breakfast, pizza for lunch, and burgers and chocolates for dinner may sound like a dream, but for your body, eating like this every day would be a nightmare. Here are some easy food tips.

EAT BREAKFAST. Sometimes it's tempting to skip breakfast when you're not hungry or haven't got time. But most food experts believe it's the most important meal of the day. Cereal, toast, and a glass of fruit juice will give you the best start and mean you're not starving by 10 A.M. and cramming cookies into your mouth.

FRUITS AND VEGETABLES. Try to eat five portions a day — and the lettuce on a Big Mac doesn't count! Instead of reaching for a slice of cake next time you're hungry, try munching a banana or an apple instead.

DRINK WATER. Food experts also advise you to drink eight glasses of water a day. It sounds like a lot, but if you try drinking it instead of soda or juice then you'll be fine. Water is good for your skin and hair and helps your body to run smoothly. Keep a bottle in the fridge so that it's extra cold!

Best breakfast

Why not try these easy and healthy ideas!

Bran cereal with sliced bananas, raspberries, and kiwi fruit
Get three of your daily fruits and vegetables in before lunch. Bananas are great at giving you energy, too, so you'll be running to school.

Freshly squeezed orange juice
If you have time, squeeze it yourself but if you're buying the carton stuff, check that there is no added sugar.

Boiled egg with whole-wheat toast Eggs are a great source of protein and, unlike frying or scrambling, boiling an egg involves no fat.

Toasted bagel with honey
Good for your sweet teeth — and honey is much better for you than sugar or jelly.

Weight a minute

Many girls worry about their weight — a result of living in a world that is obsessed with diet and appearance. This can lead to skipping meals, which is not good for your body at all. Some girls make themselves sick after meals (this is called bulimia) or don't eat at all (anorexia). These are serious illnesses that can end up damaging your health or, in extreme cases, killing you. If you or anyone you know is skipping meals or making themselves sick, then seek help immediately.

If you're concerned about your weight, the best things you can do are exercise, eat a balanced diet, and see a doctor if you think it's a real problem. Not eating at all is *very* dangerous. Likewise with crazy diets. Steer clear of them. You should only cut out a certain type of food if you're medically advised to do so — otherwise you could be damaging your body.

Five ways to love your body!

1. Stand in front of the mirror and say aloud, "I am beautiful" 10 times. You may feel silly at first but you *are* beautiful, so why not shout about it?

2. Write a list of all the parts of your body you like and pin it somewhere you can see, like next to your bed. It could be anything from "I love my smile" to "My little toe's kinda cute."

3. Learn to take compliments. If someone says they love your hair, just thank them and accept it. Don't get all shy and defensive.

4. Don't strive for the impossible. Don't waste time wishing you looked like a celebrity — without their personal trainer, personal stylist, and full-time grooming staff, they wouldn't even look like that *themselves*.

5. Accept yourself. Everyone has parts of their body they don't like, and all the things that you find annoying are what make you unique.

Ask Away!

Dear *TM*,
My older sister gets really bad pimples and it's starting to worry me. Will this happen to me, too?

Everyone is different — you may be lucky enough to get fewer pimples than your sister. You can help by keeping your face clean and moisturized with gentle products, drinking lots of water, and eating healthily. And try not to stress out — they won't last forever!

Dear *TM*,
I'm always the last one to be picked when we have team games at school. What's wrong with me?

There's *nothing* wrong with you! Your school friends may think that you're no good at sports, but you just haven't discovered which sport you're good at yet! If you haven't found the sport for you, why not try a few and find out what you like?

Boredom Busters

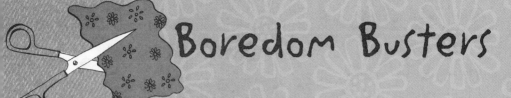

You don't have to be a scientist to **make a face mask**. You can just raid the fridge! Peel, chop, and mash together an avacado (get an adult to help you with this part) and mix it with a teaspoon of honey. Tie your hair away from your face, clean your skin thoroughly, then apply the mask, lie back, and relax for 10 minutes. Supersoft skin made supereasy!

If all those sports and exercise have left your feet feeling sore, then why not **make your own foot spa**? Fill one bowl with very warm (not boiling) water and one bowl with cold water and some ice cubes. Add some fresh mint to the warm water and put your feet in the bowl for 3 minutes. Take your feet out of the warm water and plunge them into the ice-cold bowl for a few seconds and then put them back into the warm bowl. Do this twice and it should make your feet feel all tingly. Dry your feet with a clean, fluffy towel and massage in some moisturizer or peppermint foot cream. Leave your socks off for about half an hour so your feet are properly aired out.

Get handy in the kitchen and
make a nice healthy smoothie.
You will need:

1 tablespoon honey

1 cup milk

1/2 cup yogurt

1 large banana

Mash together all the ingredients in a bowl or blender, pour into a tall glass, and decorate with a few raspberries. Mmmm!

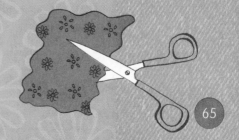

My Moments

My eyes are . . . .

My hair is . . . .

My best feature is . . . .

My fave meal is . . . .

My fave fruit is . . . .

My fave veggie is . . . .

My fave sports are . . . .

Here is a picture of me taking part in
my fave sport:

My fave athlete is . . . .

My least favorite sports are . . . .

I can swim . . . . yards.

When I'm in a bad mood, the best cure is . . . .
. . . .

I should win a medal for . . . .

If I had my own team, I'd call it . . . .

Shhh! My favorite candy is a . . . .

And here's the wrapper!

CHAPTER 5

Your personality

*A drop of ink
may make a million people think.*

Do any of your friends ever say to you, "You're so predictable!" Or do they think they know how you'd react if they told you they were gonna shave off all their hair? That's because they know what your personality is. Everyone has their own personality — it affects what we like, what we don't like, how we act, and what we believe. In just the same way that everyone looks different on the outside, we're all different on the inside, too, and our minds work in very different ways.

These are just a few of the words that we use to describe people every day. Christina Aguilera seems like a party animal and Katie Holmes seems quite calm. Think about what people think of you. You could even get them to circle the words they think describe you and see if you agree with them. You may think you're more chilled out than a cool shower but it may surprise you to know that your BFF doesn't agree!

Circle all the words that you think apply to you:

		Shy
Chatty	Nosy	Trustworthy
Crazy	Chilled out	Sensible
Party animal	Quiet	Studious
Calm	Funny	CONFIDENT
Hot-tempered	Patient	Moody

What are you like?

Take our two-minute personality test to find out what sort of person you really are....

1 You're waiting for the school bus and it's late. Do you:
A. Sigh a lot, look at your watch, and grumble when the bus finally comes?
B. See it as a chance to do some extra schoolwork and get out your books?
C. Chat with the other kids waiting at the stop?

2 You're invited to your friend's party but you only know a few people in the room. Do you:
A. Take a deep breath, smile, and talk to the girl next to you about her sparkling lip gloss?
B. March into the room, turn the stereo up, and start dancing?
C. Rush over to the chair in the corner, being careful not to catch anyone's eye?

3 What is your teacher most likely to write on your next report?
A. If she spent as much time working as she does talking, she'd be a straight-A student.
B. A good all-round student. Tries hard most of the time and gets along well with most people in the class.
C. An excellent student. Her work is always great but she doesn't make enough contributions to class discussions.

4 If one of your friends is upset and turns to you for advice, do you:
A. Let her cry, shout, and talk to you all night until you finally fall asleep?
B. Listen to her for 10 minutes, then drag her to the movies?
C. Buy a huge candy bar, give her a hug, and suggest listening to her favorite CD might cheer her up?

5 What does your bedroom usually look like?

A. Neat and tidy with every sock, CD, and book in its place.

B. Depends. Some days it's OK but others it looks like (as the 'rents would say) a pigsty.

C. Er . . . you can't remember. The place is so covered with clothes, CDs, scrunchies, and junk that you can barely find the bed.

Answers

1 A 3, B 1, C 2. **2** A 2, B 3, C 1. **3** A 3, B 2, C 1. **4** A 2, B 3, C 1. **5** A 1, B 2, C 3.

Conclusions

Wild Child (11–15)
There's nothing you love more than a party and you've got so many friends that your address book is bulging. You are confident, loud, and usually laughing. Just make sure you pay as much attention to other people as you do to yourself!

Balanced Babe (7–11)
You know when to let your hair down and when to be sensible. You love being with your buds and have a close circle of friends that you hang with. You try hard at school and with your hobbies, but you like to have fun, too. Keep up the good work.

Sensible Sista (under 7)
You always, always try your best and spend your spare time catching up on schoolwork. You are organized, calm, a good listener, and a very reliable friend. But remember that all work and no play makes us dull divas. Sometimes it's good to party and go a bit crazy, so try it . . . you might enjoy it!

The type of person you are depends on lots of things. Some of it's inherited (passed on by your parents) so maybe you've got your mom's sense of humor or your dad's impatience. Some of your personality depends on your environment. So, if you live with your mom and four sisters you may be uncomfortable around boys or if you live in a city you may be more streetwise than if you grew up in a small town. The human race is very complicated and no two people are the same. That's what makes us so interesting and confusing.

There are all sorts of interesting ideas about why everyone is different. They may not be right, but they're definitely fun. . . .

Astrology

Do you ever read your horoscope in magazines or on the Web? Well, daily horoscope readings are worked out using *astrology*. Astronomy is the science of the planets — astrology is more the theory of how the position of the planets and stars influences people. When you were born, every planet in the solar system was in a particular place and astrologists believe that this explains why people have different personalities. When people talk about your star sign, they are actually referring to where the sun was when you were born.

If you don't already know your star sign, look at the guide on the next pages and see what sign your birthday falls in. Then read up on your sign and see if the description matches you. (If you were born right near the start or at the end of a sign, you may be a little like the previous or next sign!) When you've figured out your sign and read about what you're like, here's the fun part. Ask all your friends (and your crush, if you feel confident!) when their birthdays are. Then, not only can you buy them a present, you can also work out their star sign and check out how well you should get along with each other.

Horoscope guide

Sign	Dates	Symbol	Qualities	Beware!	Friends
Aries	March 21 – Apr 20	Ram	Outgoing Generous Active Enthusiastic	Tactless Easily bored	Gemini Leo Libra
Taurus	Apr 21 – May 21	Bull	Reliable Good at cheering people up	Stubborn Holds grudges forever	Cancer Pisces Virgo
Gemini	May 22 – June 21	Twins	Friendly Romantic Loves learning	Finds it hard to be serious Can neglect friends	Aries Aquarius Sagittarius
Cancer	June 22 – July 23	Crab	Kind Protective Great listener	Clingy Loves to complain	Scorpio Taurus Virgo

Horoscope guide

Sign	Dates	Symbol	Qualities	Beware!	Friends
Leo	July 24 – Aug 23	Lion	Loyal Life of any party	Bossy Proud Controlling	Aries Libra Sagittarius
Virgo	Aug 24 – Sept 23	Virgin	Chatty Creative Sporty	Critical Opinionated Likes to gossip	Cancer Capricorn Taurus
Libra	Sept 24 – Oct 23	Scales	Charming Polite Tactful	Bad at making decisions Self-centered	Aquarius Aries Gemini
Scorpio	Oct 24 – Nov 22	Scorpion	Sociable Sensitive Sultry	Unreliable Jealous	Cancer Pisces Virgo

Horoscope guide

Sign	Dates	Symbol	Qualities	Beware!	Friends
Sagittarius	Nov 23 – Dec 22	Archer	Adventurous Fun Loves to travel	Thoughtless Unpredictable	Aquarius Aries Leo
Capricorn	Dec 23 – Jan 20	Goat	Practical Good leader Good with money	Selfish Set in ways Unadventurous	Scorpio Taurus Virgo
Aquarius	Jan 21 – Feb 19	Water bearer	Good at keeping secrets Lively	Bad temper Moody	Gemini Libra Sagittarius
Pisces	Feb 20 – March 20	Fish	Dreamy Gentle Artsy	Attention seeker Lazy	Cancer Scorpio Taurus

Colors

Bet when you choose what color dress you're gonna wear to the school dance, you don't think about what the color is SAYING! Colors can't speak, can they? Wrong! Different colors mean different things and if you have your room painted bright red instead of pale pink, not only will it be much brighter, it will also give off different vibes and say something about what kinda person you are. Here's a cool color guide:

GREEN
A calming, mellow color that will chill you out when you're stressed. Paint your room green or put a plant in there to get you feeling creative.

PINK
A warm, happy color that will pick you up when you're feeling bored or fed up. Great for your bedroom.

ORANGE
A confident color that protects against tiredness. Wear it when you need some energy.

YELLOW
An instant feel-good color. Wear it if you're feeling down and need a bit o' sunshine.

PURPLE
A very spiritual color. Wear it when you have to think deeply and are in need of a positive change.

BLUE
A trusting, reas-suring color. If it's your fave color then you are very giving and honest. Wear it and people will trust you.

RED
The color of love, passion, danger, and excitement. Wear it to show that you are totally confident and in control.

Number nuts

OK, you know your star sign, but did you realize that everyone also has a birth number? This is how you work it out. Write down your date of birth numerically. So if it's August 18, 1991, write down: 8, 18, 1991. Then add the digits up: 8 + 1 + 8 + 1 + 9 + 9 + 1 = 37. If you get a two-digit answer, add them together to get your birth number. So 3 + 7 = 10. Then 1 + 0 = 1. And here's what your birth number means:

2 OR 6

You are quiet, strong, and have just a few good friends rather than a whole gang. You stay calm under pressure and don't like to show off.

4 OR 8

You're fun-loving, loud, and a total party animal. You love watching people, always know exactly what's going on, and hate missing out on anything.

3 OR 7

You're funny, clever, and like to entertain a crowd. You love fooling around, but you're secretly a hard worker who enjoys being on her own, too.

1, 5, OR 9

You're charming, quiet, and sensitive, and you love having in-depth conversations with your friends. You're always the one your friends turn to for advice.

Dream decoder

If you've dreamed about any of the following, check out what they really mean!

SPIDERS
Someone you know is weaving a web of lies. They could be about you!

FLYING
You're doing well at school, so maybe it's time to take up a new hobby.

SWIMMING
If the water in your dream is clear, good things are about to happen to you. If the water's murky, there's a problem in your life that you have to sort out.

CATS
You are full of energy and life at the moment, and someone is watching you very carefully!

FALLING
You're upset about something and are looking for help.

It's crazy that even when you're asleep, you're actually making statements about what kind of gal you are, isn't it? Of course, all these different theories may or may not be true. As many people have believed in them over the years as have dissed them, so whether you believe or not is up to you. But you can't deny that working out birth numbers and stuff is kinda fun!

Chilled chick

If all those brain games have worn you out, then stress no more. Sometimes everyone's head needs a little relaxation. On those days when you have three hours of math, a mountain of homework, and then a piano lesson, you can often feel tired and worn out. Everyone needs to chill out sometimes. In the same way that you pamper your feet when they're sore, here are some ways to pamper your brain.

Deep breathing

You can do this anywhere. Sit in a quiet room and focus on your breathing. Listen to yourself breathing in and out. Try to breathe in for five seconds and out for five seconds and repeat this ten times. It's hard to think of much else when you're concentrating really hard on your breathing.

Massage

If you learn how to massage, then I can guarantee that you'll be the most popular girl in school, and if you give your mom a killer massage, she'll be putty in your hands (time to ask for a a raise in your allowance). Massage works by releasing tension from your muscles. Here's a basic one.

Wear comfy clothes, sit cross-legged behind your pal and close your eyes. Breathe in for five seconds, then out for five seconds to get you relaxed.

Give a head massage by sweeping your hands through your friend's hair, pressing firmly on her scalp as you do so.

Move down to her shoulders and knead them with your whole hands and knuckles. Apply pressure at the end of each shoulder.

Just make sure that before you begin a massage, the person you're massaging promises to give you one back!

Smells good

Another ancient belief is that certain
fragrances can chill you out.
Lavender oil (most drugstores sell
this) is often used in massages to
make the person feel relaxed and
de-stressed. Put a few drops in your
bath or on your pillow for a lush
night's sleep!

So if you haven't nodded off, I hope
that was a handy guide to chilling
out. We girls are often so busy shopping, chatting at sleepovers, partying,
and having fun that we forget about
ourselves. Every once in a while it's
really good to pamper yourself and
it's double the fun if you do it with a
friend. So put on your favorite CD, lie
back in your lavender bath, and take
a few deep breaths — aaaaah . . .
bliss!

Ask Away!

Dear TM,
Sometimes I just can't make decisions about anything — what to wear, whether to go to a party — whatever! How can I make up my mind without stressing?

The first thing is not to panic. If your mind is in a whirl, then you have to chill out so that you can think about things in a clear and careful way. Try to get away somewhere on your own and relax. One way of making your mind up about a party — or anything else — is to make a list of good points and bad points about that party. Is it a long way to travel? Are you going because you want to, or because you feel you should? When you've made your lists, which is longer? There's your answer!

Dear TM,
It sounds dumb, but I think there's something wrong with me. I get sooo angry all the time and I can't seem to control my temper. Whassuup?

It's OK to get angry sometimes, but it sounds like you need to try to control your anger. Deep breathing and counting to 10 are ways of calming down, as is going for a long walk to clear your head. Sports are also a great way to get rid of aggression.

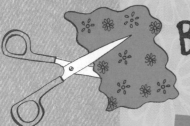

Boredom Busters

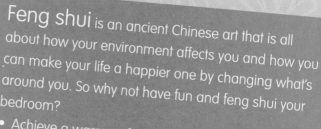

Feng shui is an ancient Chinese art that is all about how your environment affects you and how you can make your life a happier one by changing what's around you. So why not have fun and feng shui your bedroom?

- Achieve a warm, safe atmosphere by decorating your room with cream, lavender, peach, pink, red, or yellow.
- Have a large plant in the room to freshen the atmosphere.
- Make sure your bed doesn't face the door.
- Try to make sure you have space on both sides of your bed.
- Make sure your bedspread doesn't touch the floor to ensure that fresh air travels around you at night.

If you have dreams most nights, then why not **keep a dream diary**? It's best to write down your dreams as soon as you wake up, while they're still fresh in your head, so keep a pad by your bed. Then you can see if your dreams have any pattern with your real life.

Think you know what your friend's thinking or who's on the phone before you've answered it? If you do, you must have a pretty good sixth sense. Try improving your precognitive skills by trying to guess what song's going to come on the radio or MTV next. Try to communicate your thoughts without speaking by concentrating hard on something and asking your friend to try to guess your thoughts. This will develop your **telepathic skills** and you'll improve with practice. Spooky!

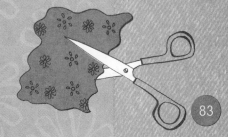

My star sign is . . . .

Star signs I get along well with are . . . .

I wish I were a little more . . . .

My friends say that I am . . . .

If I were an animal, I'd be . . . .

My birth number is . . . .

My lucky color is . . . .

This means . . . .

Here is a picture of my
lucky charm:

The last dream I had was about . . . .

When I worry I . . . .

I like to relax by . . . .

If I could make a wish come true, it would be . . . .
. . . .
. . . .

My favorite song is . . . .

It makes me feel . . . .

My favorite book is . . . .

The character I most admire is . . . .

My motto or special poem is . . . .
. . . .
. . . .
. . . .
. . . .
. . . .
. . . .
. . . .

CHAPTER 6

Your style

Be an original and the best!

Obviously, it's the person you are on the inside that counts. But the clothes you wear can also say a lot about you. The way you dress expresses your personality, affects how other people see you, and shows how confident you feel. If you know you look great, chances are you'll feel great, too. So, how do you go about choosing the right clothes for you? This chapter is gonna tell you about looking great, feeling great, and just generally being a great girl.

What's your style?

1 **When you look in your closet, what's the first impression you get?**
  A. That you've got enough sneakers to open a sports shop.
  B. Bright! Your closet contains more colors than the rainbow.
  C. Nothing really stands out, but there's lots of blue and black.

2 **How do you get ready for a party?**
  A. Try on six different dresses, find matching nail polish, and go crazy with a jar of body glitter.
  B. Take off your sweatpants and put on your jeans with sneakers and a little tee.
  C. Pull out a black skirt or trousers and a shirt or sweater.

3 **How do you accessorize?**
  A. With simple jewelry and a little bag.
  B. Glitter, neon, leopard skin, denim . . . you'll try anything!
  C. Er . . . what?

4 **If you were given some money for your birthday, what would you buy?**
  A. A cool denim jacket you've been wanting for ages.
  B. A new top, some cute hair clips, and lip gloss.
  C. A new pair of sneakers.

5 How long do you spend styling your hair before you go out?

   A. Hours and hours — you've almost worn out the carpet in front of your bedroom mirror.

   B. You go for a sleek, straightforward look that takes a few minutes to achieve.

   C. A few seconds is all it takes to give your hair a quick shake — you prefer the just-got-out-of-bed look!

Answers

Conclusions

Party gal (11–15)

It's the brighter the better for you. You love to make an entrance when you walk in the room and your clothes reflect this. You love keeping up with the latest trends and accessorizing your outfits.

Safe 'n' stylish (7–11)

You go for practicality and comfort over glamour. Your closet is full of classic items that will never go out of style, like black trousers, plain tops, and shirts. You always look sophisticated and stylish.

Sporty sista (Under 7)

As long as you're comfortable, you're not too bothered by what the fashion experts are saying or whether Adidas stripes are in this season. You love tank tops, sweatshirts, and, boy, do you love sneakers!

Ten wardrobe essentials

No matter what style you go for, there are some things every gal needs in her wardrobe.

1. **JEANS.** You can never have too many pairs of jeans. Wear 'em stylish with black boots or casual with sneakers or sandals.

2. **BLACK PANTS.** They never go out of fashion and they look great, too.

3. **DENIM SKIRT.** Long or short, in the summertime there's nothing you'll get more wear out of than a denim skirt. Cool and pretty.

4. **SNEAKERS.** OK, so they're totally fashionable but they're comfy, too. Great for hanging out in town or at the park.

5. **PAJAMAS.** 'Cause when you're ill or just feeling a bit sorry for yourself, there's nothing better than having a bubble bath and changing into your PJ's.

6. **PARTY DRESS.** This is great if you get invited to a party at the last minute and have nothing new to wear. Go for something simple — you can always brighten it up with accessories.

7. **SLOGAN TEE.** Wear one to reflect what mood you're in! They're great ways of getting attention without saying a word.

8. **HOODED SWEATSHIRT.** Keeps you warm when it's cold and hides your hair if you're having a bad day.

9. **SWEATPANTS.** Like, what else are you supposed to wear to slouch around the house in?

10. **SPARKLY TOP.** Ideally a nice, brightly colored one that you can wear with jeans or a skirt to give you a bit of glam 'n' glitter.

"I love bargain-hunting. You can get some real bargains and original clothes from secondhand stores."
Emma (12)

Fashion on a budget

Coming up with all the things you should have in your wardrobe is one thing, but what if your piggy bank's emptier than your lunch box after school? Don't worry, you can still look great even if the loot is running low.

Real Deals

Secondhand shops are great for finding cool stuff that you can guarantee no one else will have — and they're cheap! The stuff always looks worn, too, which is way trendy now and also means that jeans are nice and soft and the denim looks faded. Guilt-free shopping. What more could a gal want?

Swap shop

If you and your best friend are roughly the same size and shape, one of the cheapest ways of getting new clothes is to swap them! You might be bored with that sparkly T-shirt, but your friend will love to look a bit different! It's probably best to check with your mom and dad before you do this. Also, if you're not sure you want to say good-bye to those purple flares forever, you could always lend them to your friend just for the weekend.

Customizing

This is one of the coolest rediscoveries of the last 10 years. Look closely in the stores and you'll find new stuff that looks as though it's been customized with bits of lace, beads, and badges. So why not just save your pennies and do it yourself? Get yourself a glitter pen and a pair of scissors and get creative. Customize jeans by fraying them or sewing patches on the back pocket. Tees are easy to jazz up with pieces of lace or by cutting the neckline and making it jagged. You can even customize jackets and bags by putting a few cool badges on them. It's all about being creative and letting your personality shine through, so you can be as wild (or not) as you want.

Some easy looks

Are you the kind of gal who flips through magazines but doesn't know what style to go for? Do malls dazzle you with choices? Here are some types of looks for you to copy. Fashion made easy!

Skater gal

Big 'n' baggy is where you're at and even if you can't skate, this look is always ultratrendy. Jeans should be flared and tees should be fun. Retro cartoon characters printed on them are good. Hair and makeup should be quite plain, but you could accessorize with some sweatbands. Layering is essential (long-sleeved tees under short-sleeved tees) and sneakers should never, ever leave your feet.

Essential look — Flared blue jeans or cords, a brightly colored tee over a long-sleeved white tee, a woolly beany hat, and a chain going from your front to back pocket.
Celeb example — Avril Lavigne

Hippie chick

Long and flowing is the name of the hippie-look game (and this applies to your hair, too). Colors should be girly and pretty — pink, baby blue, and pale yellow are all good. Accessories are easy for this look; just pick some flowers from the garden and put them in your hair. If your hair's long enough, put it in two braids and tie flowers around the bands.
Essential look — Long flowery skirt, sandals or flip-flops, a pretty vest top, and some wooden beads. Thread daisies through your hair and even around your wrist if you're good at making daisy chains.
Celeb example — Nelly Furtado

College cool

Being a college gal is all about being retro (wearing things from a few years ago). Funky sneakers are good, and worn jeans and old school baseball tops and caps complete the look. Wear your hair in a high ponytail and carry a cute bowling bag and you'll look straight outta high school.

Essential look — Faded jeans with a few rips in them, a sporty old-fashioned '80s football or baseball top, white sneakers, and a bowling bag.

Celeb example — Katie Holmes

Garage gal

Extravagance and glamour is right up your street. Garage gals like to look like they're going to a party 24/7 and their fave colors are black and gold. Jewelry's gotta be gold, too, and hair should be sleek 'n' straight or big 'n' bouncy.

Essential look — Black dress, black shoes or glittery sandals, fake leopard-skin bag, and plenty of gold jewelry.

Celeb example — Mis-Teeq

The cool thing about style is that one day you could be a hippie chick and the next a skater gal. Who says you have to stick to one?

Confidence and how to project it

Clothes can make you feel like you're a proper princess and totally great. On the other hand, if you feel uncomfortable and think your new purple top is just a little too bright, then clothes can make you feel awkward and embarrassed. So it's important to make sure you feel comfy in whatever you buy. Feeling good in what you wear is a way of projecting confidence. Turn the page for some other ways:

MAKE LOTS OF EYE CONTACT.
Looking down at your feet makes you look awkward and uneasy, but hold someone's gaze and you'll look really sure of yourself.

WEAR RED. It's true — red is a color that is associated with power and boldness. Even if you hold a little red bag or wear a red hair clip and bangle it will show people you mean business

STAND TALL. Bad posture and slouching is not only bad for your bones, it makes you look frightened, too. Try holding your shoulders back, keeping your chin up, and making sure you keep your back straight. Practice walking while balancing a book on your head. It's an old-fashioned idea, but it works.

DON'T FIDGET. Although it's really tempting to twirl with your long hair or the tassels on your jacket, try not to. This makes you look really nervous.

SPEAK UP. Don't shout, but make sure you're not mumbling. Use your hands and body movement while you're talking to express yourself more. It's good to be animated and lively and it will keep the people around you more interested in your stories, too.

Shopping for your shape

As we already know, like the best box of chocolates, gals come in different shapes, sizes, colors, and varieties. Some clothes look better on some shapes than they do on others. Here's a guide.

1 Ruler-shaped (tall and slim, with narrow hips)

Go for:
- Small prints (gingham, plaid, or floral).
- Frills and pleats.
- Baggy pants with low waists.

Stay away from:
- Low-cut tops.
- Tops and bottoms in the same color (makes you look longer).
- Lycra leggings with big, clumpy shoes.

2 Triangle-shaped (broad shoulders and slim hips)

Go for:
- Baggy pants.
- White skirts and pants.
- Vest tops (to show off your fab shoulders).

Stay away from:
- V-neck tops.
- Cropped jackets.
- Horizontal stripes.

3 Short stuff (narrow shoulders, with short legs)

Go for:
- Vertical stripes (you'll look taller).
- Shoes with a little heel.
- Little cardigans and cropped jackets.

Stay away from:
- Long, baggy clothes.

4 Curvy (big shoulders and broad hips)

Go for:
- Scoop-neck tops.
- Baggy pants.
- Darker colors.
- Knee-length skirts (better for curvy legs than miniskirts).

Stay away from:
- Low-waisted pants.
- Frills and bows around your neckline.
- Cropped tees.

95

Made up!

Style isn't just about wearing the right clothes. Hair and some fun makeup are just as important. No one wants to wear six layers of makeup and look like Christina Aguilera onstage — and too much of it is bad for your skin. Besides, we're beautiful anyway — we just need a few finishing touches on special occasions to make us feel a bit more glam.

Skin

It's important to keep your face clean and fresh — a gentle soap or face wash is all you need to look great. If you're gonna wear a little makeup for a party, then ask if you can borrow a little light makeup remover to take it off afterward.

Sparkly eyes

Keep your eyes as natural as you can. Avoid too much eye makeup, as this can make them look smaller and might smudge horribly! On special occasions, a touch of sparkly eye shadow looks great. Apply from the corner of the eye (nearest to the nose) outward with a sponge brush. A touch of Vaseline on the lashes looks just as good as mascara — and is easier to wash off!

Lush lips

The easiest way of looking lush for a party is to make your lips sparkle. There are lots of different lip shines, sticks, and glosses that are nice 'n' natural rather than making your lips tomato-red. When you're not wearing gloss, remember to keep your lips moisturized with lip balm.

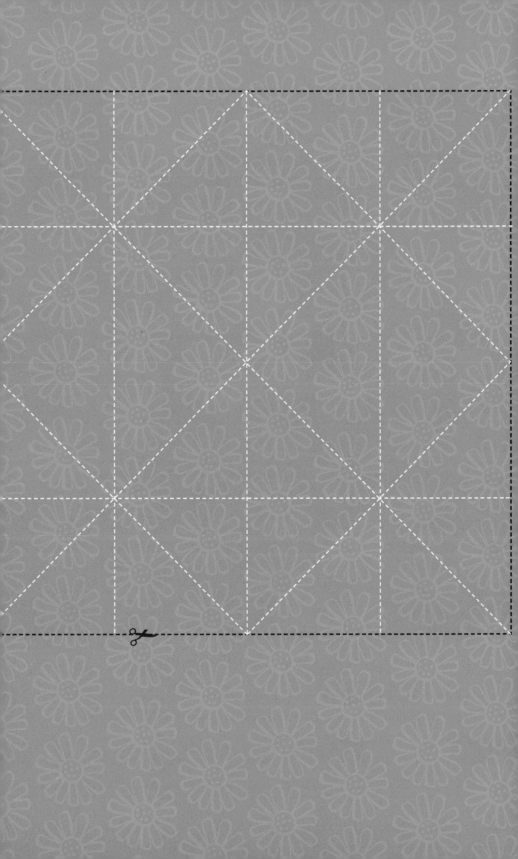

117 + 118

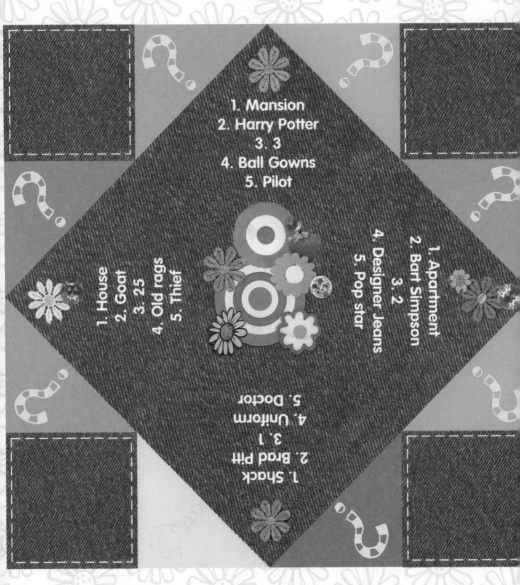

1. Mansion
2. Harry Potter
3. 3
4. Ball Gowns
5. Pilot

1. Apartment
2. Bart Simpson
3. 2
4. Designer Jeans
5. Pop star

1. House
2. Goat
3. 25
4. Old rags
5. Thief

1. Shack
2. Brad Pitt
3. 1
4. Uniform
5. Doctor

fortune-teller

Pull out this page and then cut out your fortune-teller. Follow the instructions on h
to put it together on page 117. See how to use your fortune-teller to play M.A.S.H.
page 118 and learn about your future!

ISBN C-R19-551048

Do the laundry

Do my homework

Read a book

Eat a chocolate bar

Watch TV

Paint my toenails

Your Decision Maker

Pull out and carefully cut out your decision maker cube. Fold up the sides and join up the edges. Stick down with glue or sticky tape.

SBN C-R29-551048

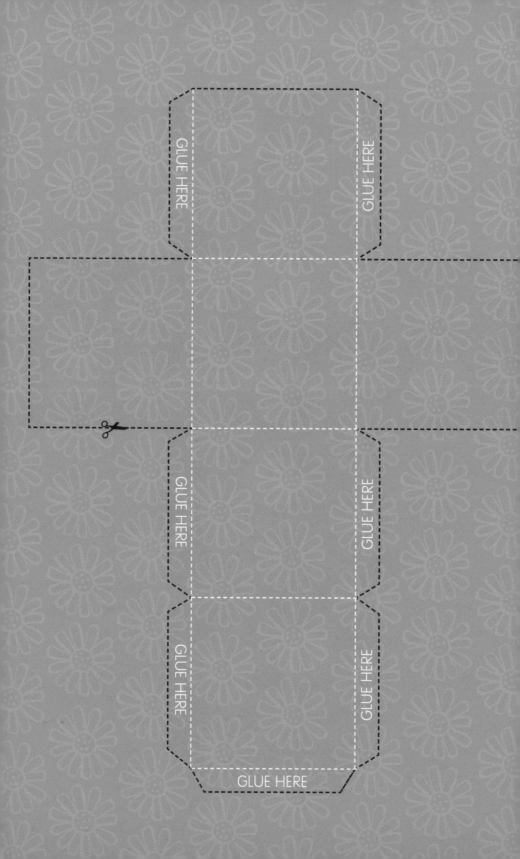

GLUE HERE

GLUE HERE

GLUE HERE

GLUE HERE

GLUE HERE

GLUE HERE

GLUE HERE

Suits you!

There are sooooooooooo many colors of eye shadow, lipstick, and mascara to choose from that it's easy to get confused. Here's a handy color chart that's perfect for sleepovers, to see which colors will suit you best.

Brown eyes	Mocha, brown
Hazel eyes	Pink, red, auburn
Blue eyes	Peach, gold
Green eyes	Lilac, purple, pink

Let your fingers do the talking

Work out what your fingers and nails say about you:

Long fingers — *You are creative and hardworking. Don't overdo it and neglect your friends.*

Short fingers — *You're kind and caring but need to think before you speak.*

Long nails — *You're a good judge of character and often guess what your friends are thinking.*

Short nails — *You're a born worrier,* *but that's only because you care about your friends so much.*

Nail it

One of the most common bad habits among us gals is biting our nails. If you want to stop ('cause let's face it, half-chewed nails look pretty ugly), then try using the special polish that tastes bad when you chew your nails. If you pamper your nails and start to like how they look when they're clean and polished, maybe you'll want to grow them longer. Finally, don't feel alone — girls all over the world bite their nails.

Once you've got your nails a nice length, it's time to decorate them! If you're going for just one shade, remember to apply the color in a stripe down the center of the nail and then go on either side. You could be really adventurous and make patterns with different colors of nail polish. Remember to let the first coat dry properly before you add other colors (or it could get mega-messy!) and keep a bag of cotton balls handy to mop up any mistakes. If you do wear nail polish, make sure you remove it once a week and *never* pick it off.

If nail polish isn't for you, then how about getting some nail stencils? They're stickers for your nails and look really cool, even if your nails aren't so long. You can get lots of different designs, they're not as much hassle as polish, and they look really cute.

DIY beauty

Save money by making your own beauty products:

- Vaseline makes great mascara and lip balm!
- Mashed bananas are really good for dry skin.
- Strawberries and plain yogurt mixed together make a fab mask for oily skin.
- Squeeze the juice of a lemon on to your hair after you've washed it. Then let it dry in the sun to bring out natural highlights.
- Put some apple cider vinegar on your hair after it's washed to bring out any red highlights — prepare for it to smell a bit, though!

So there you have it. Your total style guide. The trick to being a fashion guru is not to try too hard (or if you have tried hard, to make it look as though you haven't). Apart from the fact that it's bad for your skin to be caked in makeup every day or for your feet to be crammed into heels all the time, dressing up is best done sparingly. If you look as though you're going to a dance every day, then when you *do* go to a dance, you'll just look normal.

Find a style you feel comfortable with, that really suits you and sums up your personality, but don't be afraid to experiment with different looks. And when it comes to makeup, less is more — right? Get it? Got it? Good!

Ask Away!

Dear TM,
My mom won't let me choose my own clothes. All of my friends buy really trendy stuff for themselves, but Mom picks "sensible" things for me to wear. What can I do?

Your mom is probably worried that if she buys trendy clothes for you, you'll only wear them a couple of times before they go out of fashion. Have a chat with her and see if you can reach a compromise — and find something to wear that you both agree on. Your mom doesn't want you to look frumpy — she just doesn't want to have to buy new clothes for you every week. And you don't have to go for really trendy clothes. Just pick something that suits you and you'll look cool!

Ask Away!

Dear *TM*,
I hate my hair. It's just sooooo curly and it won't do anything I want it to do. Help!

First, no one is ever happy with their hair and I bet if you had really straight hair, you'd be wanting to get some curl and bounce into it. Anyway, curls are totally in at the moment. Christina Aguilera, Britney, J-Lo, and Sarah Michelle Gellar have all tried out the curly look. Curly hair can be hard to handle, but it can also look spectacular! Next time you get your hair cut, ask your hairdresser for some tips on how to keep your curls under control.

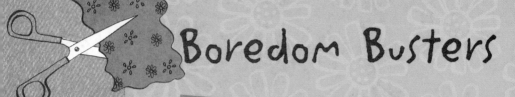

Boredom Busters

Customize a funky tee. Cut a row of strips about 1 inch wide and 6 inches long at the bottom of the T-shirt so you get a pretty fringe effect. Then thread a bead through one of the strips, tie it so the bead won't fall off, and do this randomly around the tee. You could even do it on the sleeves. Finally, stitch around the neck of the tee and add a bead every second stitch to make the whole top sparkle.

Perfect skin recipe. Follow this every day and your skin will stay soft and smooth all year-round:

- Eat tons of fruits and veggies.
- Drink eight glasses of water a day.
- Get at least eight hours of sleep a day.
- Wash and moisturize daily.
- Only use ultraclean and soft washcloths and towels.
- For tired eyes, lie back with some cold teabags, apple slices, or cucumbers on them for 10 minutes.

Make sure your hair is always shining with this

hair mask:

- Crack 2 eggs into a bowl, add 2 teaspoonfuls of olive oil, and the juice of half a lemon. Mix together until well blended.
- Rinse your hair with warm water and towel dry.
- Stroke the mixture through your hair and massage it into your scalp for a few minutes using gentle, circular movements.
- Sit down, relax for 10 minutes, then rinse the conditioner out of your hair and shampoo it as usual.

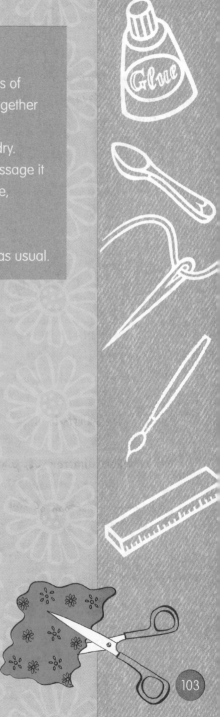

My Moments

Here is a picture of me wearing my fave clothes:

My style is . . . .

My favorite hairstyle is . . . .

My last hair disaster was when . . . .

And here's a cartoon of me!

My most precious piece of jewelry is . . . .

My fave shoes are . . . .

My fave item of clothing is . . . .

Clothes that suit me best are . . . .

I don't like wearing . . . .

My fave shop is . . . .

If I were a movie
star, I would wear
this outfit
to the premiere of
my new film:

My style icon is . . . .

CHAPTER 7

Your spare time

Time flies when you're having fun!

How many times do you find yourself muttering these two little words? *I'm bored*. It's usually on a Sunday after-noon when there's nothing on TV or during summer vacation when you've run out of your allowance and are so bored you even find yourself asking the 'rents if you can do anything for them! Well, fear not, in this chapter we're gonna tell you just how many cool things there are to do in your spare time. After all, we've only got two days off school a week — we'd better make the most of them!

Get creative

Put your spare time to good use by making something. You can do this alone or with your friends. And you can keep your inventions or give them away as presents!

"I love making things. It makes you feel good when you make some-thing cool and different."
– Fiona (9)

Craft box

Keep a box in your room filled with pieces of fabric, cards, glue, sequins, glitter, beads — in fact, don't ever throw anything away! Then, when-ever you're bored, you can use these bits and pieces to make a hundred different things! Try making jewelry holders out of shoe boxes, birthday cards with glitter on them, cushion covers out of fabric and beads . . . the list is endless! You could even decorate the craft box itself!

Become an author

Have you ever read a book or story and thought that you could do a better job? (Hopefully not this one!) Well, why not give it a try? Think up some characters, give them names and personalities, dream up a few storylines and get writing. It's what J. K. Rowling did — and look at her now! If you think of yourself as a romantic poet, then sit outside — in the garden or in a park — so nature can give you some inspiration! And if you've written something that you're really proud of, send it to your local newspaper or the school magazine. Even national magazines are always on the lookout for new writing talent.

Picture perfect

Ask if you can borrow a camera from your folks, or pick up a disposable one — they're quite cheap. Then get snapping! You could take photographs of your family, your friends, scenery, animals — anything you like! Looking at photos is great fun and the more practice you get, the better you'll become. You could even end up as a swanky photographer for a magazine and get to meet all the celebs! Once your pictures have been developed, you could make cool picture frames out of cardboard and give them away with the photos as presents.

Drawing diva

If you're good at art and always doodling, why not keep a sketchbook? Then, when the mood takes you, whip out your colored pencils and get drawing. It could be an object in your room, a view, a picture of you, or something totally from your imagination. You could try designing clothes or drawing a dream house.

Just dough it!

Here's a quick 'n' easy recipe for making clay, which you can use to make buttons, badges, ornaments, and pendants. Take equal amounts of sliced bread and runny glue. Crumble the bread, then add the glue and mix it around. If it's really dry, add a splash of water. If there's any food coloring in the kitchen cupboard, add a bit of that, too. Then mold away, making shapes, but be careful not to hold the clay in your hand too long because it will turn crumbly. When you're happy with your shapes, leave them in a cool

room for an hour to dry. When they're dry, coat them with hair spray or clear nail polish to give them a bit of gloss.

Webwise

Instead of using the computer just to surf Websites (which is guaranteed to keep you occupied for a few hours), why not try making your own site? It's a great way of learning, showing the world what you're interested in, and making new friends.

Reuse, recycle, redesign

Customizing is the way forward — it extends your wardrobe and shows that you're a totally unique, creative *chica.* So don't throw out that old pair of jeans — turn them into funky shorts! Brighten up that old tee by sewing on some lace or getting artsy with a glitter pen. Customizing is perfect for us 21st-century gals — it's all about recycling and making the most of our environment.

Get earning

Why not put your week-ends to use and earn yourself some extra cash? You should ask the 'rents first, but with any luck they'll be so desperate to stop your moping around the house they'll agree with these moneymaking ideas:

Dog walking

Ask friends and neighbors if they want their dog walked for a small fee. It keeps you fit, gets you out and about, and fills your pocket. While we're on the subject of pooches, pets are great boredom busters. If you've got a pet, you can play with it, walk it, train it, groom it, and make it learn tricks! If your parents won't let you have a pet (and they do take a lot of looking after), then maybe a neighbor has a pet that you can play with. Does your school have a pet that you can take home over vacations? If you prove how good you are at looking after someone else's pet, maybe your parents will change their minds after all!

Car washing

OK, it's hardly glam, but washing cars with a friend can be fun. Start off with your parents' car, then ask other people on your street if they'd like their cars to be clean and shiny, too. Grab yourself a bucket and cloth and keep your fingers crossed that it does-n't rain!

Face painting

If you're a sure hand with a makeup brush, then buy yourself some face paints. Tell friends and family that you're available for kids' parties and charge a couple of coins for a lion or a clown face. Better practice on some willing volunteers first — a younger brother or sister will do.

Get sporty

Swimming
There are tons of things you can do in a pool besides swimming. Water volleyball, water aerobics, and water polo are a few examples.

Racket sports
Round up a friend who's as bored as you, then hit the local recreation center or park for a game of tennis or badminton. If that sounds a little too energetic, then Ping-Pong is just as much fun.

Dancing
Whether you prefer ballet, jazz, or tap, there's bound to be a class near you that will teach you the right moves. All you need is a leotard and tights, some comfy shoes, and you're on your way!

Skating
Skateboarding, ice-skating, and roller-skating are all great hobbies — they're fabulous exercise, too.

Biking
Bikes can be used for more than just a trip to the local shop. Join a BMX club, buy yourself a helmet, and the sky's the limit!

Ball sports
Basketball, volleyball, soccer, and baseball are all great team games. If your school doesn't have sports clubs, maybe you can join a local team or start your own. Before you know it, you'll have a whole team of friends!

Martial arts
It's never too early to start learning how to defend yourself. Sports like kickboxing, judo, and karate are good for body and mind, but if you ever run in to any trouble, they will also help you look after yourself.

"I just love running, riding my bike, and swimming. It's fun and you get a good night's sleep 'cause you're so tired."
Fiona (10)

Volunteering

There are probably lots of places in your neighborhood that are desperate for helpers. Whether it's dog walking at a kennel or cleaning the litter out of the local river for an environmental group, it's great to do things for other people and your community. You'll meet people *and* feel good about yourself.

"I like joining clubs. It means that I get to meet other people who like the same stuff as me."

Jody (12)

Get socializing

Taking up a new hobby is a good way of finding new friends. Or maybe you and your gang are bored of watching videos all the time. . . . Here are some ideas.

Band

If you take lessons at school or privately, then you may be good enough to join a band. If your school doesn't have one, maybe there's a youth orchestra nearby that you can join. You'll get to put on shows and even go traveling around if your band's really good. And, with you in it, it's bound to be!

Theater

Consider yourself the next Kirsten Dunst? If you think that you could hack the Hollywood lifestyle and are serious about acting, then a local theater group could be for you. Find out if your school has a drama club or check out local theaters in the Yellow Pages. You'll learn all about acting and the theater and get to put on plays. You may even be discovered by someone in the crowd. . . .

Party planner
Why not spend your spare time doing something *really* cool like planning a party? You could make it a pop-star party or even a Barbie party and design your own invites. Then you could make a mix tape, write a guest list, and even plan some party games.

Camper girl
Camping outside is great fun (as long as it doesn't snow), so why not get a group of friends together and try to get your hands on a tent, sleeping bags, pillows, blankets, a flashlight — and chocolate! Ask if you can camp in someone's backyard and spend the night gossiping, playing games, and telling spooky ghost stories.

These are just a few ideas of the many things you can do, but I bet you can think of more. Write them all down in the *My Moments* section, then whenever you're getting bored, read this book for instant ideas. Having a hobby is a great way of learning, meeting new people, and keeping fit. There's a whole world out there — what are you waiting for?

My Moments

Here is my very best boredom buster! . . . .

. . . .

. . . .

. . . .

. . . .

. . . .

My best-ever party was when . . . .

. . . .

We ate . . . .

. . . .

. . . .

We watched . . . .

We danced to . . . .

We stayed up until . . . .

If I could write a book it would be (circle)

Funny   About real-life

An adventure   A mystery

A fairy tale   Sad

Exciting   Magical

I would call it . . . .

My author name would be . . . .

My favorite computer game is . . . .
. . . .

My favorite funny movie is . . . .

My favorite scary movie is . . . .

I almost cried watching . . . .

My favorite CD is . . . .

I love dancing to . . . .

If I were in a girl band it would be called . . . .
. . . .

CHAPTER 8

Your fortune-teller

How to make your fortune-teller

Try making your fortune-teller, and then test it out on your friends!

1. Ask an adult to help you cut out your fortune-teller on the printed page inside this book.

2. Place it facedown (dotted lines up). Fold the square in half, then in half again, and unfold. Then bend each corner into the center, as shown.

3. Turn over the square. Then fold all four of these corners into the center, as before.

4. Fold it in half. Then fold it in half the other way. Put your thumbs and first two fingers into the pockets at each corner. Your fortune-teller is now ready!

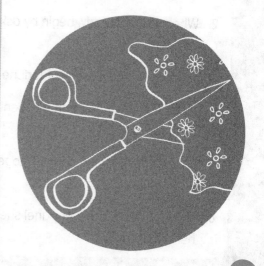

Learn answers to these five big questions about you and your friend's futures!

1. Where will you live?
2. Who will you marry?
3. How many children will you have?
4. What kind of clothes will you wear?
5. What sort of job will you do?

1. Pinch your thumb and forefinger together, then open and close your fingers and thumbs. This is the movement you need to work the fortune-teller!

2. When you are ready, begin by asking your friend one of the five questions.

3. Then open and close your fortune-teller until she says, "Stop."

4. Next, spell out her name by opening and closing the fortune-teller, as before.

5. For example, for the name "Imogen" you will have to open and close the fortune-teller six times.

6. Finally, open whichever panel she picks and read out the answer to her question.

My Moments

Here's a space for you to add your special moments....

My Moments

My Moments

My Moments

My Moments

My Moments